Health, Safety, and Environmental Regulation

How Effective?

John Charles Daly, moderator

Mark J. Green
Howard M. Metzenbaum
James C. Miller III
Alan K. Simpson

Held on July 30, 1980
and sponsored by
the American Enterprise Institute
for Public Policy Research
Washington, D.C.

This pamphlet contains the edited transcript
of one of a series of AEI forums.
These forums offer a medium for
informal exchanges of ideas on current policy problems
of national and international import.
As part of AEI's program of providing opportunities
for the presentation of competing views,
they serve to enhance the prospect
that decisions within our democracy will be based
on a more informed public opinion.
AEI forums are also available on
audio and color-video cassettes.

AEI Forum 44

ISBN 0-8447-2199-9
Library of Congress Catalog Card No. 80-70492
Printed in the United States of America

JOHN CHARLES DALY, former ABC News chief and forum moderator: This public policy forum, part of a series presented by the American Enterprise Institute, is concerned with the effectiveness and efficiency of the social regulation enacted in the 1970s as a response to the protests and the turmoil of the 1960s. Our subject, "Health, Safety, and Environmental Regulation: How Effective?"

This discussion will focus inevitably on the major social regulatory agencies, the Environmental Protection Agency (EPA), the Consumer Product Safety Commission (CPSC), the Food and Drug Administration (FDA), the National Highway Traffic Safety Administration (NHTSA), and the Occupational Safety and Health Administration (OSHA).

The birth or strengthening of these programs in the early 1970s—OSHA was born in 1970—reflected a broad consensus on the seriousness of the problems. It assumed that the cost of regulation to the public and the private sectors would be more than matched by the benefits to society. By the mid-1970s, concern surfaced that these programs imposed burdens, particularly with respect to their impact on the economy. President Ford instituted the inflation impact statement early in his administration. It required the executive branch agencies to prepare evaluations of the expected impact of all major new regulations on prices, productivity, and competition.

In 1978 President Carter refined this approach in the Improving Government Regulations Program. This program required the executive agencies to prepare regulatory analyses of all regulations expected to have an annual effect on the economy of $100 million or more. These analyses were to include major alternatives and a rationale for choosing one over another. President Carter mandated regulations which "shall achieve legislative goals effectively and efficiently and shall not impose unnecessary burdens on the economy."

Thus, an earnest search began for a cost-benefit formula. This produced passionate argument on both sides of an issue that is described by the Center for Policy Alternatives at the Massachusetts Institute of Technology (MIT) as "a new art form that is still in a primitive state of development." In a March 1980 study contracted by the Senate Committee on Governmental Affairs, the MIT center states, "Estimating the benefits of regulation is an extremely complex, analytical task for which appropriate data and models are often unavailable. Furthermore, there are serious problems associated with attaching values to such intangibles as injury, chronic disease, death and pain and suffering."

We have a highly expert panel to lead us through this labyrinth, seeking a reasoned balance between human benefit and economic necessity. Mark J. Green is the former director of Congress Watch; he is an associate of Ralph Nader; and he serves on the Clean Water Action project and the Citizen Labor Energy Coalition.

Senator Howard Metzenbaum serves on four Senate committees, Budget, Energy, Judiciary, and Labor and Human Resources.

Senator Alan K. Simpson is a member of the Judiciary, Environment and Public Works, and Veterans' Affairs committees.

James C. Miller III is codirector of the Center for the Study of Government Regulation at the American Enterprise Institute and is an AEI resident scholar.

To begin, gentlemen, I would pose the same question to each of you, in turn. Are the social goals of the 1960s being achieved by the legislative and regulatory responses that were enacted in the 1970s?

HOWARD METZENBAUM, U.S. senator (Democrat, Ohio): We are making good progress. There are problems of overregulation, there are problems of learning how to deal with some of the new programs. Without question, there is too much paperwork.

In the 1960s, we learned that the air we breath is not clean and the water we drink is not clean. We learned that industrial accidents are killing more people on an annual basis than we lost in the entire Vietnam war. We have made some changes, though not all of them have been good; not all new products that come to market are good.

Let's take a look at our present situation. The 1981 cars will be 95 percent lower in emissions than the 1967 models. One 1967 car put out as much pollution as twenty 1981 models. Ten years ago, the lake that is near where I live, Lake Erie, was dead. Nobody could swim in it, nobody could fish in it. This year sportsmen will catch over 3 million walleyes. I was delighted to drive past Lake Erie the other day and see people, lots of people, swimming in that lake.

Crib safety standards were abominable in the 1960s. New crib safety standards have reduced injuries to infants by 44 percent since 1974. Life expectancy averaged 69.7 years in 1960. It is pushing 74 years in 1980. We have made some progress. Medicaid, prenatal care, and pediatric care have had an enormous impact on infant mortality. In 1965 the infant mortality rate was forty per thousand. Now it is down to about a third of that, about fourteen per thousand.

We have made some headway, but we have a lot of mountains to climb and a lot of problems still to be conquered.

ALAN K. SIMPSON, U.S. senator (Republican, Wyoming): The regulatory agencies have failed to do what they intended to do. How can anyone argue with air quality legislation, water quality, pollution controls? All of those things are extraordinarily and eminently worthwhile. We still do not weigh the cost/benefit of regulation, but we will have to pay some serious attention to that.

The issue is that Congress has labored along, and the American citizen thought the job had been done. Measure by measure, and piece by piece, there has come to be a solid wall of burdensome regulation that has preempted the prerogatives and the control of state and local government on every issue. Although these programs originated in a worthwhile idea, they failed because they were hatched in an area of compassion fatigue in America, which has left us still limp. Apparently we believe that the best method now is simply, as they used to say in the eighteenth century, to let the brooding omnipresence of the law be the finest and strongest environmental measure. Americans deserve a lot better than that.

MARK J. GREEN, former director, Congress Watch: The goals have been met. We must realize that the goal is to reduce injury and to avoid death in the workplace and marketplace. To appreciate this purpose, I think you have to understand what inspired it in the workplace and in the marketplace. The Cuyahoga River caught fire in 1970, and rivers are not supposed to catch fire. One out of eleven workers had a reportable injury or disease in the late 1960s. There were 30,000 product-related deaths, most avoidable, according to a national commission in the late 1960s. In 1906, Upton Sinclair wrote *The Jungle,* a novel about the stockyards and what was put into our food. Thalidomide was manufactured, not here, as a result of action by the Food and Drug Administration, but abroad, in the early 1960s. The situation at Love Canal in New York is not an aberration. There are thousands of such cases around the country, according to the Environmental Protection Agency.

Government regulation, in a sense, is government at its highest purpose. It is the exercise of the police power to protect citizens against illegality and abuse. We certainly understand this exercise of the police power as it relates to crime in the streets. We should also appreciate government exercise of this police power as it relates to crime in the suites.

If the death rate per mile driven were the same today as it was in 1966, instead of 50,000 deaths a year there would be 80,000 deaths a year. Thirty thousand Americans are not dying every year because of government regulation.

Senator Metzenbaum spoke of the Consumer Product Safety Commission ruling on cribs. By ensuring that crib slats are a certain maximum distance apart, the ruling has reduced by half the number of infant deaths from crib strangulation. This affects me not only as an advocate, but as a parent of a seventeen-month-old daughter.

The problem was not that these manufacturers were bad people; the problem was that companies were afraid to be at a cost disadvantage if they did something special. The result is that the manufacturers wait for a government regulation insisting on safety so that all manufacturers suffer the same cost, and then the benefit can be distributed massively throughout society. The only problem is that government regulation in many areas should be strengthened, not weakened or diluted.

JAMES C. MILLER III, codirector, AEI Center for the Study of Government Regulation: Some of the regulatory objectives have been accomplished; many have not. Unfortunately, many of the objectives that have been achieved were obtained at extraordinary costs. Many programs have had either no benefit or even negative benefit.

We need to focus quite clearly on this regulatory phenomenon, because it has mushroomed in size. It has grown manyfold since the early 1970s when the major initiatives were undertaken.

At a time when the economy is in a downturn, when people are concerned about jobs and productivity, questions about the adverse impacts of regulation need to be addressed very critically.

Estimates have been made about the costs and the benefits of regulation. My colleague, Murray Weidenbaum, has estimated that the aggregate cost is some $100 billion per year. I estimated that just the new carcinogen standards that OSHA is likely to promulgate will cost on the order of $55 billion a year. We may quibble over the exact amounts. But those are large numbers, or, as the late Senator Everett

Dirksen used to say, "A billion here and a billion there, and pretty soon it adds up to real money."

The question is, are we getting the biggest bang for our buck? Are the existing programs serving the public well? Could they be improved by critical analyses of the type that many of us have advocated—analyzing the benefits, analyzing the cost, making trade-offs as appropriate, and emphasizing not only who gains from regulations, but who bears the costs.

MR. DALY: Unquestionably, we are in a time when there is a questioning as to the amount of government that is imposed on our people.

Dr. Miller, while public opinion polls show most people in favor of less regulation in general, they also show that the public wants more, not less, regulation to achieve specific health and safety goals. How do you reconcile these findings? What implications do you think they have for regulation?

DR. MILLER: They offer a challenge to the social regulators to improve the decision-making process and thereby the quality of their decisions. Some of the agencies, unfortunately, simply put blinders on and assume that the pursuit of zero risk is the appropriate objective. But we all know that zero risk is not achievable. The Supreme Court recently pointed this out. When we stand out in the sunlight, we increase our risk of cancer, but sunlight is good for us in other ways. There are trace elements that are necessary to human life that are also carcinogens. Agencies must look at these trade-offs and make intelligent decisions about them. When they do that better, they will gain the confidence of the general public.

MR. DALY: Dr. Miller has referred to the Supreme Court decision. I assume you were referring to the benzene case.

DR. MILLER: Yes.

MR. DALY: Who would like briefly to outline and comment on the benzene case?

SENATOR METZENBAUM: I do not want to speak to the Supreme Court decision, but I would like to speak to some other remarks of Dr. Miller.

MR. DALY: Fine. We will come back to it later.

SENATOR METZENBAUM: You mentioned Dr. Weidenbaum's figures. The fact is that he has been compiling those figures over a period of years. In the past, about 42 percent of that total cost came about not by reason of the regulatory process that protects the public, such as the EPA, OSHA, and FDA standards. About 42 percent of the cost resulted from higher consumer prices resulting from tariff protection against imports and from price and entry regulations by the Interstate Commerce Commission (ICC), the Civil Aeronautics Board (CAB), and the Federal Communications Commission (FCC).

If you want to join with me and indicate that you think there ought to be more trucking deregulation, fine. I believe there ought to be free competition in the trucking industry. Congress has already said it will deregulate, and it has deregulated, the airline industry.

With regard to the Federal Communications Commission, the American people would look favorably on any kind of idea that would make it possible for more to enter radio and television markets. But the fact is that the American Enterprise Institute, which is the promoter or the sponsor of this program, does not come forward and say, let's do something about the ICC and the CAB and the FCC. We only talk about EPA, things that protect the public, and about OSHA, things that protect the working man. As a matter of fact, industrial accidents are another subject. They cost the nation $15 billion last year.

I agree that regulation may have gone too far. Congress has already indicated that it is concerned about too much regulation. The Regulatory Reform Bill, of which I am a cosponsor, came out of the Judiciary Committee. A Regulatory Flexibility Bill has come out of the Government Operations Committee. We must make some changes. Let's not, however, put all the burden on some of these agencies that have made it possible for more people to be living on a healthier basis today. We ought to give credit where credit is due.

DR. MILLER: May I respond to that, Senator Metzenbaum, by saying that I certainly agree with the thrust of your argument about the reform of ICC and CAB regulation. In fact, I personally have written widely in that area, advocating reform, and I have testified before Congress to that effect. Also, I should mention that the American Enterprise Institute has published a number of volumes analyzing the inefficiencies of that kind of regulation.

In my view, your committee, under Senator Kennedy's leadership, is to be commended, along with Senator Cannon and his committee, for pushing through the airline regulatory reform bill and also the trucking regulatory reform bill. Those are quite important initiatives that will benefit the economy and people generally.

Let me respond now to your comment about other bills. The bill before the Congress requiring regulatory analyses of proposed regulations is very peculiar. Most laws are subject to judicial review. This bill says that agencies must do regulatory analyses, but whether they do them, and the extent to which they rely upon them in their decision making, is not subject to judicial review. It gives complete discretion to the agency.

SENATOR METZENBAUM: I am not arguing about the specific merits of the bill. What I am saying is that we, in the Congress, recognize that there needs to be some improvement in the overregulation of the American public. I am concerned that too many people would like to throw out the baby with the bath water, that they want to abolish the whole program. I am not opposed to improving the regulatory procedures; I am only concerned about how far we

DR. MILLER: Right.

SENATOR SIMPSON: You speak of risks in society. What I hear, and the theme is always the same, is an association of risks with horror stories. There is never anything we deal with in the Congress that does not have a horror story attached to it. And if anyone objects, or has the temerity to challenge or to comment on that horror story, he is considered Neanderthal, a clod, an uncaring human being, and various other things that are associated always with consuming guilt. I don't buy that. So I just wade right into the issues.

We spoke of people who have been spared and who no longer die from environmental causes or workplace accidents. Certainly—that's great. Now they are dying of frustration; they are covered up with rules and regulations, and they have no confidence in us. If we in Congress think that we are elevated beyond some other elements of society, we are very wrong. The people have no confidence in us, have no confidence in the regulators, and they are in an ugly mood, as I perceive it. I have talked to colleagues who are coming back from the campaign trail, Democrats and Republicans alike, and reporting that the electorate is really hostile.

Howard Metzenbaum talks about figures and challenging figures. How about the figures on the national budget that we got in January, which were wholly revised in March, which were wholly revised in May. Then we had a balanced budget eight weeks ago, and now we are $31 billion in the hole. That is the way they play with figures around here.

MR. GREEN: A federal health safety regulation is probably responsible for perhaps 1 percent of the federal budget. We could have a panel on the federal budget. Those few health and safety programs cannot be blamed for the federal budget deficit.

You implicitly criticized horror stories. Let's talk not of them, but of buzz phrases. Dr. Miller talked about a zero-risk society. Of course we are not aiming for zero risk; we cannot eliminate sunlight. That's really a straw person.

It was possible to eliminate an underarm spray deodorant propelled by fluorocarbons. Individually, it was a banal, boring product; collectively, it threatened the only ozone layer this planet has. So big government regulation told industry to take the fluorocarbons out of aerosol sprays. The industry protested that it would be too expensive; it would put companies out of business. The government was not blackmailed; it insisted on the rule. The day the rule went into effect, pump sprays came on the market, and they were cheaper; the ozone layer was no longer threatened.

Let's talk about the $100 billion Dr. Miller mentioned earlier. At least 25 to 30 percent of that amount is paperwork that is required by the Internal Revenue Service. We may not like the Internal Revenue Service, but that revenue-generating function is not what we would call regulation. That $100 billion figure is an example of what I call Chicken Little economics. It is an exaggeration to scare the government and the public into thinking that government is too expensive. For example, that $100 billion includes the cost of installing the buzzer interlock in cars. That was an idea proposed by the Ford Motor Company. Congress reversed that law, yet that $100 billion still includes that cost.

We must be very careful about the estimates of the cost of regulation and the estimates of the benefits. Who controls the data, the cost data, about regulation? The companies being regulated control that data. If a policeman asked a speeder if he were speeding, he would probably say he was not. If we ask a business about the cost of regulation, the business may tend to exaggerate.

One further example. Vinyl chloride, a known carcinogen, was threatened with regulation by OSHA in the mid-1970s. The vinyl chloride industry protested that regulation would cost 2 million jobs and $60–90 billion. The industry was regulated, with no loss of jobs and at a cost one two-hundredths of that estimate.

DR. MILLER: I would like to respond to the question of business having control over data. That is true to a large extent, although the businesses report data to the federal government. The source of much of our data for determining whether a regulation should be imposed comes not from the companies that would be regulated but from the regulatory agencies. The raison d'être of a regulatory agency is to pass regulations. There is, therefore, a bias on the part of an agency—not in every case, but as a general proposition—to show that a regulation is more likely to achieve its stated objective than perhaps is warranted.

Often we tend to compare an imperfect marketplace with a theoretically ideal, perfectly operating regulatory agency. My friend Roger Noll once said that economists spent the first forty years of this century identifying market imperfections that would justify regulation and have spent the last forty years identifying imperfections in regulation that cry out for deregulation or for a return to an albeit imperfect marketplace.

Talk about benefit-cost analysis is not simply a call for reducing regulation. One side of benefit-cost analysis is to say that we can achieve the given benefits for lower cost. The flip side is that, for the same cost imposed upon society, we can achieve more benefits of the type that most of us would agree are reasonable.

SENATOR SIMPSON: Let's take a look at the so-called Bumpers Amendment legislation, which is having an excellent bit of success in the Senate and the House. It is a very simple issue. It says that the regulations of the federal government shall no longer be entitled to the presumption of validity in a court of law. It must have pretty good support from the majority party to get passed, of course. The support results from the frustration percolating through from the citizenry. This propensity to exaggerate—good heavens, no one has a corner on that market.

One of the other interesting things with regard to the study is, whose figures do you believe? That subject may be fully probed as the result of a proposal by Senator David Pryor, a Democrat from Arkansas, and Representative Herb Harris, a Democrat from Virginia, who are investigating the consultation process and the contract process. The consultation process is a very simple one. A government agency hires consultants to do a study; the consultants like eating so much, they tell the agency exactly what it wanted to hear. If we have to work with figures resulting from that sort of process, then we are all making a tragic error.

SENATOR METZENBAUM: I would like to say to my good friend from Wyoming that I have no problem in zeroing in with him on the use of consultants, which is probably one of the greatest wastes of money in the federal government. It is unbelievable. The Department of Energy spent something like $8½ billion out of a $10 billion budget for consultants, which is just absurd.

Returning to Jim Miller's comment about regulation or deregulation. Deregulation is a very popular term. The president deregulated the price of oil on a phased-out basis. The executive branch told the people it would only cost $16 billion. Now the executive branch has told us it will cost $49 billion over a two-year period. That is inflationary. That hits average working people in the pocketbook, where they have the most difficulty coping with it. It has to do with heating oil, it has to do with gasoline.

We must make a distinction. There are some regulations that are good; there are many regulations that are bad; and there are many regulations that find that middle ground. I am concerned that too many people would like to throw regulation out altogether. That is where the real problem lies. Certainly there is too much regulation, and there is too much paperwork. Having said that, exactly what changes do we advocate, either as individuals petitioning the Congress or as members of the Congress.

MR. DALY: That is what we should come to grips with.

Dr. Miller, you made the point that the analyses in President Carter's programs do not allow benefit-cost analyses to be reviewed by the courts. How would judicial review of these analyses improve their effectiveness?

DR. MILLER: Judicial review would improve the effectiveness of those analyses because it would cause agencies to take them very seriously. Agencies do not take the analyses very seriously today because they know that nothing will happen to them if they do not. Nothing will slow down the pace of their regulatory process. If there were judicial review, and an agency either proposed a regulation that was grossly excessive in cost versus benefits or failed to propose a regulation where the identifiable benefits were much greater than the cost, someone in the private sector could obtain relief from the courts. If agencies realize that they must meet certain standards or they will not be successful in promulgating regulations, they will begin to meet these standards.

My fellow panelist Mark Green is absolutely correct: benefit-cost analysis is no black box, it is not perfect. I argue, however, that benefit-cost analysis, subject to judicial review, would mean a significant improvement in the performance of the regulatory agencies. It would increase the benefits to society of the things that they do, and it would reduce the costs.

MR. GREEN: Any rule or regulation issued by an agency is now reviewable if someone wants to take it to court, or to Congress. So if a cost-benefit analysis that leads to a rule or regulation is not reviewable, the rule or regulation itself certainly is.

Like so many aspirations of society, cost-benefit analysis works well in concept, but it works terribly in practice. The House Oversight and Investigations Committee said that the most important thing about a cost-benefit analysis is the name of the sponsor. If a company is doing it, the company has an instinct to exaggerate. Further, many benefits are not measurable by numbers. We know that it is better to be able to see across the Grand Canyon than to see pollution. What is the dollar value of that?

Do we know exactly the dollar value of avoiding cervical cancer in the daughters of women who today ingest DES (diethylstilbestrol)? We know there is a rough correlation between DES and cervical cancer. We do not know it exactly. In this particular case, there is a thirty-year time lag between ingestion of the hormone and development of cancer in the next generation. Economists cannot calculate that.

A monetary value must be placed on a life. Some studies say life is valued at $300,000, another study says $2 million. One of the methods for calculating this is called discounted future earnings; that is, if someone loses their life, what would they have earned over their lifetime. This is a serious methodology. The problem is that it values far more highly a white stockbroker from Scarsdale than a black domestic. That is morally unacceptable. It is, apparently, economically acceptable.

This cost-benefit analysis is a greatly flawed methodology right now. If imposed today, it would automatically prejudice government against issuing regulations that lead to avoidance of injury and disease, to often unmeasurable aesthetic and recreational gains. It prejudices the whole process. We should respect cost-benefit analysis, improve it, but not burn incense to it by locking it into the government today when its analytical value is in great dispute among economists of both sides.

SENATOR SIMPSON: Mr. Green talked about not going to horror stories, but he just related three of them. Maybe you do not realize that, in each of these issues, you addressed the area of a horror story. That type of emotionalism has put us where we are.

I remember the maxim "Emotion will always triumph over reason, but reason will always persist." That is where we are right now. The people of America are demanding reason.

MR. GREEN: Which horror story? Give me one and tell me if it is a true story or a representative—

SENATOR SIMPSON: You mentioned the Grand Canyon, and you mentioned DES, and—

MR. GREEN: Are those untrue?

SENATOR SIMPSON: They are horror stories. That is the issue. Let me finish, then you can have a crack at me.

Here is an issue, right here. We are in trouble with energy in America because we do not have energy security. Our president is crying for production of coal. Where is the coal? Right out there in the state of Wyoming and in the state of Ohio. We are not going to be able to develop that. We have not even started to fight, but we will be fighting about eastern coal versus western coal, union coal versus nonunion coal, high-sulphur coal versus low-sulphur coal. The fight will be on; we will never get the job done. The issue always comes down to the fact that there is a horror story in the background. If we favor reducing federal regulations so coal can be mined on federal lands, then we are responsible for papering America with acid rains from tip to tip.

DR. MILLER: I think what Mr. Green described is a bad benefit-cost analysis, not a good one. I would not necessarily ascribe to that methodology.

Perhaps more important is his contention that benefit-cost analysis provides an automatic bias against benefits and in favor of costs. There are benefits that are not easily measured, but let's not forget that there are costs, too, that often do not enter a benefit-cost analysis—things like innovation. Perhaps the most important, one that I think is too little considered today, is the cost to individual freedom. A lot of regulations impinge on individual freedom, yet benefit-cost analyses seldom take that into account.

SENATOR METZENBAUM: On this question of freedom, we are all in favor of freedom, we all believe in the American flag, and apple pie is good, too. But is it freedom for a worker to have the privilege of working in a plant where he has a 90 percent chance of being exposed to one of 163 dangerous toxic chemicals? Is it freedom for people to pollute the Love Canal and then to walk away from it and say they did not advise the residents because they knew the residents would be upset? Is it freedom to sell an infant formula that causes many children to be injured permanently? Is this the kind of freedom that we are talking about?

What we are really talking about is providing some kind of protection. Because one corporation sold a faulty infant formula in this country, for about eighteen months, many children will pay for the rest of their lives. That is not the kind of freedom that I think the American people envisioned when the Constitution was put together. It is not the kind of freedom that the American people are looking for at this moment.

MR. DALY: Let's see what we might look for in the future. One widely publicized instance of regulatory reform is the Environmental Protection Agency's so-called bubble concept, under which a company is allowed to reduce pollution from all sources added together, rather than reducing pollution by a specific amount from each source. What is your view of this and of other reforms of similar character instituted by the EPA?

MR. GREEN: I would like to see that kind of market-oriented experimentation on a selective basis. It cannot be imposed industrywide, because it is untested. But if the result of a test is beneficial, and less costly, fine. We have only been ten years into the kind of health and safety programs that are the subject of this panel, and they were instituted, by and large, during a Republican administration, continued by a Democratic administration.

There is a great consensus in this society for health and safety regulation. There is a consensus against the abstraction called regulation, but for the specific programs that Mr. Daly cited in poll data. Certainly I would like to see experimentation. I am sure it could be improved as the process evolves.

MR. DALY: Another proposal for solving the problem of so-called orphan waste sites, waste dumping sites whose owners are not known and for which there is no one to pay a clean-up bill, is to create a super fund to be used for cleaning up these sites. What is your view of that proposal, Senator Metzenbaum?

SENATOR METZENBAUM: Where would the super fund come from? If it is just federal funds, I would not be in favor of that.

MR. DALY: That is considered, and also making industry contribute to such a fund.

SENATOR METZENBAUM: I am not sure that a factory located in San Francisco ought to be responsible for contributing to cleaning up the waste in Pittsburgh, Pennsylvania. There might be some equitable basis on which that could be determined. Frankly, however, if it means higher taxes, or if it means putting the budget more out of balance, then I do not favor it.

SENATOR SIMPSON: Is that a promise?

MR. DALY: Do you want to talk to that one?

SENATOR SIMPSON: No—yes, I would. [Laughter.]

SENATOR METZENBAUM: I am glad we got you to change your mind.

SENATOR SIMPSON: I was deeply involved in the super fund idea. I started with the premise that all of us right here would start with: I thought we ought to do something about orphan dumps; we ought to develop a way to deal with them. If it cost $300 million or $400 million to do that, we should do it, we should take care of those dumps, either through high temperature incineration or whatever. We ought to do it, we ought to audit the sites, we ought to make the states get into it.

MR. DALY: One of the most popular legislative proposals on Capitol Hill over the last few years has been the legislative veto. Would the legislative veto be an effective means of achieving better regulation?

SENATOR METZENBAUM: When the Federal Reserve Board drives savings and loan associations out of business and makes it possible for commercial banks to pay the same interest rates on savings as do the savings and loans; when the Federal Reserve also provides tight money and causes increased unemployment in this country; when it drives up interest rates and, as a consequence, adds to the inflationary pressure, then I would favor a legislative veto.

Interestingly enough, however, nobody proposes a legislative veto for the Federal Reserve Board or for any of the agencies that

I would say are business oriented. A legislative veto is always proposed with respect to the Environmental Protection Agency, the Federal Trade Commission, a consumer-oriented agency, and a number of other agencies that are more related to the public and to the consumer.

The legislative veto would open a Pandora's box. Today one group of legislators may get a legislative veto in for EPA and FTC regulations, and then that Congress will change, and we will be vetoing the decisions of the Securities and Exchange Commission, and the Federal Reserve Board, and some of the banking agencies—the Comptroller General, the Federal Communications Commission.

The legislative veto is a very dangerous invasion of the executive department. We ought to let the executive branch do its job, and then there ought to be an appropriate appeal to court, should that be desired. Legislative veto looks good to me on certain days, but generally speaking, I do not think it is good policy.

DR. MILLER: I would certainly agree with Senator Metzenbaum. I think the legislative veto is a very bad idea. It is a bad idea first, because of the constitutional issue that my colleagues at AEI have raised and are very concerned about. Second, it would spread the locus of adversary activity from within the agencies to Capitol Hill. Congressmen and senators have more important things to do than to think about the specific issues before regulatory agencies.

Furthermore, these veto resolutions would be packaged. They would be voted on en masse. So congressmen and senators would be voting on good vetoes and bad vetoes at the same time. Whichever way they voted, they would be using a meat ax instead of a scalpel.

All told, the appropriate approach is to change surgically each of the regulatory statutes, to give the agencies more direction about what they should no longer do and what they are not doing now that they should do. Legislative veto is an imperfect tool for achieving this.

MR. DALY: Another proposal concerns regulatory budgets. Each of the regulatory agencies would be given a budget that it could expend for its enforcement actions. When it ran out of money, it would have to stop for that year. What do you say to that?

MR. GREEN: Absolutely terrible idea. Suppose it runs out of money the day before massive documentation comes forward of the kind of toxic dump sites that we all are so worried about? Also, the regulatory budget is not really based on out-of-pocket expenditure by an agency, which is measurable, but on the compliance cost by the industry. The agency is dependent on industry's assertion for that figure. It would be in the interest of the industry, therefore, to inflate the numbers, so the regulatory budget would be spent very quickly. It is a device to eliminate the kind of health and safety regulation that was the purpose of these agencies in the first place: to reduce injury and avoid death in the marketplace.

DR. MILLER: May I say that the regulatory budget is an excellent idea. It would force agencies to establish priorities, to choose among the alternative regulatory initiatives those that would give the biggest bang for the buck. The agencies would have to plan over the year's horizon; they would have to decide when they were going to promulgate regulations; and they would have to choose among them.

With the possible exception of the question of how easy it is to quantify off-budget costs, all the arguments that could be made for a regulatory budget are precisely the arguments that are made for a financial budget. Suppose the Congress had no financial budget. We would know very little about how individual programs were to be financed, from whom the revenues would come. That would be chaotic. One reason we have something bordering on chaos in many areas in regulation is that agencies are not forced to think in terms of limited resources and of setting priorities.

MR. DALY: We have talked about the cost of regulation, and we have disagreed about the usefulness of cost-benefit analyses in making decisions about regulation. We have said some things cannot be measured as costs, such as the restrictions on personal freedom, or as benefits, such as the value of human life and suffering. We have explored a few alternative ways of achieving benefits, such as the bubble concept of controlling air pollution, the super fund that would be used to clean up waste areas, legislative vetoes, and regulatory budgets.

Now let's get to the views and the questions of our experts in the audience. May I have the first question, please?

CALVIN COLLIER, former chairman of the Federal Trade Commission: My question concerns a series of proposals, apparently gaining popularity in the Congress, known as proposals for two-tiered regulation. Under these proposals, small businesses would have regulatory standards in such areas as health, safety, and the environment that are different from those that apply to large businesses. What are your views on this form of two-tiered regulation? Do you think two-tiered regulation would produce for the public the most bang for the buck, as Dr. Miller mentioned earlier?

MR. GREEN: In some instances, I like the idea of requiring less reporting—for example, statistical data reporting—from small businesses, because they are small. The economies of scale are such that it would be very arduous for them to report the kinds of things that Exxon can report. But in the health and safety area, we would have to be very careful. Life Sciences was a tiny subsidiary of Allied Chemical, and because it put an insecticide, Kepone, into the James River, it would today cost $8 billion to clean up the James River. A small business, large result.

SENATOR SIMPSON: The two-tiered system is workable. We should recognize the difference between a business with a great number of employees and a business with fewer than ten employees. We must keep that distinction in mind. We must also keep in mind the safety records of those businesses. We can find that out easily as a result of the workmen's compensation laws, which exist in every state in the union. Pull the trigger on that employer, look at his record under the workmen's compensation law. If he has not had an accident or a draw on his fund, let him off the hook.

MR. DALY: Dr. Miller, would you define the procedures that would apply to businesses with fewer than ten employees? We have not really explained this proposal and the two-tiered system yet.

DR. MILLER: Various proposals are floating around. One of them would leave small businesses alone, unless there were some evidence they had a problem.

MR. DALY: Small businesses being those with fewer than ten employees?

DR. MILLER: Some proposals place the limit at larger sizes. Essentially, however, the proposals suggest leaving small business alone unless there is substantial evidence that they were performing poorly with regard to the health and safety of their employees.

Under the proposed bills, however, I understand that if a particular employee feels that the working conditions are unsafe or unhealthy, he or she may petition OSHA, and OSHA would then have authority to inspect the premises.

SENATOR METZENBAUM: I support the concept of dealing with small businesses in a manner that differs from dealing with the larger corporations. I accept the two-tiered approach. I do not, however, support any suggestion that small businesses be exempted from regulations that protect the lives and the health and the welfare of their employees. The lives of the employees of small businesses are every bit as important as the lives of employees of larger businesses. If the two-tiered approach is used to eliminate a lot of the paperwork and a lot of the statistical data, however, then it does make sense.

ROBERT ZENER, Washington attorney: My question is addressed to Mr. Green. Do you oppose cost-benefit analysis in all situations? Specifically, there are many situations in which the cost of an environmental regulation is, in itself, a harm to the environment or to health. For example, it is obvious that the net impact of nuclear regulation has been to discourage, indeed, almost to stop, the building of new nuclear power plants. As a result, new power plants burn coal. That means miners are killed or injured mining that coal, and there is a substantial environmental cost in burning coal: acid rain, for example.

MR. GREEN: Nuclear plants are not being built because they are uneconomical. I like the idea of a regulatory official asking: What benefits do we aspire to in this rule? How many lives could we save? Where? How many injuries could we avoid? What are the potential costs? What are the competing uses of the money that we would spend on this regulation? This is rational and, indeed, required under law. Unless there is a reasonable basis in fact, a rule or regulation could be struck down by a court for being arbitrary or capricious. That kind of cost-benefit analysis is absolutely necessary. It is called logic. It is unrealistic to think that there is any mathematical formulation that can prove that the benefits exceed the costs by a dollar or more. That is not achievable in the real world. If that is imposed by law, as a bill proposed by Senator Robert Dole attempts to do, it will threaten the destruction of health and safety regulation.

DR. MILLER: Mr. Green brought up the amendment by Senator Dole. I support that. Again, the issue is not that the science of benefit-cost analysis is so precise that we can provide answers that everyone will agree on in every case. The important thing, however, is that we will make substantial advances in the performance of the regulatory agencies.

We would also eliminate much of the silliness that accompanies many regulatory initiatives. The National Institute for Occupational Safety and Health, for example, has just published a list of toxic substances that regulatory agencies are to be concerned about. On that list are oxygen, salt, pepper, and other commodities that we use every day.

Many things provide some kind of risk, but we must not devote the nation's resources to types of risks that are so far down the priority list that they are not worth thinking about. To the extent that we should be devoting the nation's resources to reducing risk, we should be putting the highest priorities first. That is what benefit-cost analysis is all about.

RICHARD PATTERSON, Dow Chemical Company: I address my question to Mark Green. You like cost-benefit in some instances, and you dislike many of the other regulatory reform proposals that have been presented. You agree, I believe, that there is a degree of overregulation. How would you propose that we eliminate or at least significantly reduce the overregulation that we all agree is there and the costs that go along with it?

MR. GREEN: I was an early supporter, actually, of the regulatory analysis impact bill proposed by Senators Abraham Ribicoff and Charles Percy, which is working its way through the Senate. I like the idea of more public participation programs in the agencies.

Right now, if the Federal Trade Commission has a proceeding on hearing aids, the industry, of course, will be there. But people who use hearing aids can also be there, because they are given small amounts of money, since they cannot afford lawyers and scientists on their own, to make a case before the regulatory judges. The Federal Trade Commission, though, is unique. We need more of those programs at other agencies so both sides can be heard.

We also need more congressional review—not legislative veto, but the kind of congressional oversight in which Congress has been negligent.

Now I am going to abuse my prerogative and say two sentences about horror stories. I plead guilty to using them. Of course, I will call them evidence, not horror stories. I use them because they are representative, and I use them because I find that the criticism from

Senator Simpson is always abstract. Paperwork is bad. Overregulation is bad. But as long as the critics of horror stories go up the abstraction ladder, I am going to insist on talking about the real people who are injured from pollution and marketplace abuse. Is that undue passion? I plead guilty to that.

SENATOR METZENBAUM: I would like to add an additional comment. The gentleman who asked the last question is associated with Dow Chemical, and that is fine. But we really ought to recognize that, in this country, as of this moment, the chemical manufacturers—and Dow is certainly one of the bigger ones—have opposed regulation of toxic chemicals. We face a real tragedy in the country. The EPA estimates that 46 million tons of toxic waste are generated each year, and 41 million tons of that, about 90 percent, are improperly disposed of. Much of that waste comes from chemicals.

In Michigan, 90 percent of the population has been exposed to PCB (polychlorinated biphenyl) contained in chemicals that became mixed up with livestock feed. As a consequence, they have to worry every day of their lives about what the future holds for them.

Perhaps we all ought to be thinking not about whose ox is being gored, or who is on one side and who is on the other side. I think it is time for the manufacturers, the chemical manufacturers and others who are involved with dangerous substances, to come forward and work with us in government to provide protection for the public, without, at the same time, providing burdensome regulations. That is what really ought to be coming out of this meeting.

SENATOR SIMPSON: I understand what Mr. Green is saying. He and I have shared a podium previously. I do not always agree with him, but he certainly is enthusiastically supportive of his prejudices.

MR. GREEN: Yes, that's it.

SENATOR SIMPSON: He uses the term evidence but I still refer to it as high drama. That is precisely where we get in trouble. He is talking about human beings, and that is exactly who I am speaking about. I am speaking of human beings in those states, who are absolutely fed up with the procedures that overwhelm them. Those are the things that Howard Metzenbaum mentioned when he asked about freedom. Is it freedom to put your windowsill forty-two inches above the floor? Is it freedom to have a stretcher at a one-man coal mine? Is it freedom to have 767 pages of permits to drill an oil and gas well on federal lands? When those things do not happen, human beings are affected.

SENATOR METZENBAUM: Those are pretty good horror stories.

SENATOR SIMPSON: I knew you would say that! What we really come to is that anyone would really believe, staying in Washington long enough—and I hope I don't—that the states are run by clods, but that is not the way it is. States are run by legislators who are Democrats and Republicans and who pass OSHA laws and workmen's compensation laws and safety laws, and they do that all the time. But you would never believe that here.

DR. MILLER: The argument for public participation is based on the false premise that the agency typically is an objective judge and hears evidence only from the business community. The agencies, by and large, are not objective judges, but pursue their own objectives; and those objectives are sometimes counterbalanced by the evidence put forth by the business community—especially in the health, safety, and environmental areas. There is some argument that the old economic regulatory agencies that Senator Metzenbaum spoke about earlier—the Interstate Commerce Commission and the Civil Aeronautics Board—were captured by the industries they regulate. But industry certainly has not captured OSHA or EPA. They are truly adversaries.

The second point I would like to make is that the question of lives is very important. What we find often, however, is that regulations do not promulgate reductions in the probability of loss of life, but, in fact, increase it. The American Enterprise Institute has published many studies that raise significant questions about the rate of innovation of new drugs. Because of the scares from thalidomide and other drugs, officials at the Food and Drug Administration have an extraordinary reluctance to approve a new drug. If they approve a new drug and it turns out to be harmful, then everyone knows it and they catch the dickens for it. On the other hand, if they hold up approval of a drug that would save many lives, no one knows about it. So there is an asymmetry in their response to these regulatory initiatives.

MR. GREEN: If the FDA has cost more lives than it has saved, would you urge its abolition?

DR. MILLER: If it has cost more—

MR. GREEN: You have asserted that it costs more lives than it saves because of drug lag. Would you urge the abolition of it?

DR. MILLER: If that were true in the aggregate, I surely would.

MR. DALY: I don't believe he said it cost more lives; he said that there was a balance to be struck.

SENATOR METZENBAUM: Dr. Miller, you talk about whether these regulations do any good, and whether we ought to have them. OSHA inspections led International Harvester to spend $1.3 million on safety improvements alone at a Wisconsin foundry. Earlier this year, the foundry reached 1 million worker hours without a lost-time accident. Harvester now admits that it would not have spent the money had OSHA and the union not forced the issue. More important even than that is the fact that the company says its return is fewer accidents and greater productivity.

We are not talking just about cost; we are talking about saving lives. We are talking about $15 billion a year in industrial accidents, which represents ultimately a cost to the American consumer. We are talking about the intangibles that Mark Green mentioned, such as the value of eight or ten or fifteen rivers around the country, that have been cleaned up by EPA regulations and are again usable by the public. That is an intangible cost. I do not know what it is worth to see some kids swimming in Lake Erie, but it is worth something.

DR. MILLER: Yes, it surely is. Most of us would certainly laud the kinds of regulations that result in benefits that are substantial in relation to the costs.

Let's look at an example of the opposite, however. Let's say that a firm's machinery is producing noise above the level at which workers would sustain hearing impairment. OSHA says the firm must install engineering controls—baffles mounted on rubber footings and enclosures—to reduce the level of noise. In areas where the level of noise is excessive, workers wear personal protection devices—earplugs or earmuffs. Engineering controls cannot always reduce the level of noise to within safe limits. Yet OSHA says even if the engineering controls will not be effective, the firm must install them. In that case, the workers still wear the earplugs. The workers are no better off, they are no more protected. Yet the company—its stockholders and its ultimate consumers—pay dearly for totally wasteful regulation.

SENATOR METZENBAUM: I do not know the specifics of that situation, but there may be instances in which bureaucrats overregulate. I have no difficulty in joining with you in challenging it.

I hope that you will join with me, then, in support of OSHA regulations, for example, on asbestos exposure. Those regulations will ultimately save about 2,500 lives a year from lung cancer. We cannot overlook the fact that the Surgeon General has estimated that 20 percent of all cancers may be related to carcinogens encountered in the workplace. Without OSHA, without this monster governmental agency doing something about industrial accidents and chemicals in the workplace, many employers would go on subjecting their employees to risk. I know that there are many employers who would be doing the right thing and would be very much concerned. But there are a host of employers who would not. It is the employees of those employers about whom we must concern ourselves.

DR. MILLER: Senator Metzenbaum, I join you in urging that those kinds of cases be dealt with, but dealt with extraordinarily rationally.

SENATOR METZENBAUM: I agree.

SENATOR SIMPSON: All these things that we have discussed were great, there is no question about it. And what has happened to them? They are being administered by overzealous persons who have worked their way into the regulatory process and who bring their own personal prejudices with them.

I want to reiterate one thing, which Mark Green has heard me address before: the issue of intervenor funding. I favor intervenor funding, for example, to an individual who has been cheated on his hearing aids. I do not favor giving the Americans for Democratic Action about $200,000 to come and testify at intervenor hearings on such issues as health spas, ophthalmic goods, and the funeral industry. That is what is happening to intervenor funding. It is being abused. It goes to groups that have their own high constituency—that have a large dues-paying membership. That is wrong.

CHARLES STEADMAN, chairman, Steadman Security Corporation: It has been suggested here that when regulatory agencies are considering any particular action, it would be appropriate for them to take into account the relative costs and benefits. It is also an established fact that regulatory agencies tend to operate by their own rules, chosen as they proceed along their course of action. In view of these circumstances, how can the American people be assured of a certain and consistent application of a cost-benefit standard in the absence of mandatory legislation?

MR. GREEN: There was an article in *U.S. News and World Report* last year that asked regulators if they felt that they were recklessly on their own, having an impulse to regulate everything in sight. And the regulators responded, because that was the prevailing cliché, "Are you kidding?" When the regulatory agencies propose a regulation, the industry, which is always interested, can sue. Members of Congress, like Senator Simpson, who watch this process with the eagle eyes of their staffs, can insist on congressional oversight, if not legislative veto. There is now a procedure suggested for presidential veto. It is remarkable; the regulators cannot do anything on their own, much less regulate the kinds of carcinogens that we would suggest be regulated. Regulators now are constantly being watched by government at all levels. If Congress does not pass a mathematical cost-benefit bill such as the one proposed by Senator Dole, there are a lot of safety valves built into the process so that the agencies will not make bad regulations.

One last thing. Though government is not perfect, as Senator Simpson said, I still trust the cop on the beat more than the person driving the car. We need cops on the business beat trying to crack down on business illegality. They may make mistakes, but if we leave it to the marketplace, we will be back to 1906, when Upton Sinclair wrote *The Jungle.*

SENATOR SIMPSON: That was before we had a Sherman Antitrust Act. We seem to have forgotten all that. That is all on the books. I always am fascinated to see these new pieces of antimonopoly legislation come up. Good heavens, we already have a structure of antimonopoly legislation on the books that would choke a horse.

There must be legislation to reduce the regulatory impact, without question. I also favor the legislative veto. I have heard all those stories that it cannot work, that it will overwhelm Congress. It really does send a message out, however.

SENATOR METZENBAUM: I would like to say a word for all of those horrible bureaucrats. They are people. They really are not such evil people. They are working for a living, and they are trying to do a good job. Many of them are very dedicated public servants, probably earning much less than they could earn in private industry. Certainly, some of them go overboard, but so do some business people, so do some labor union leaders, so do some people in the Congress, and maybe in the executive office, as well.

Let's find the problem, zero in on the problem, and find the solution. But let's not whipsaw every government employee and think he is evil, per se.

DR. MILLER: As a former bureaucrat, myself, I could not agree with you more. Bureaucrats, as Senator Humphrey said in an AEI Public Policy Forum once, have mothers and fathers, too, and many are devoted and work very hard—including the next questioner, Dr. Broder, from the Council on Wage and Price Stability, I believe. [Laughter.]

IVY E. BRODER, formerly of the Council on Wage and Price Stability, now at American University: Although you talked briefly about the bubble concept, I wonder if any of the members of the panel would like to give their opinion on some other economic approaches to regulation, such as effluent charges, noise charges, and so forth.

SENATOR SIMPSON: The bubble concept will be a great thing. For the first time, we will not only get the emission from that plant in the bubble, we will get the dirt from the road that people have been driving on for about eighteen hours during that day. We will get an authentic reading that we do not get when an agency is out to shut down a plant and does not separate what is happening at the plant from the other areas that are just normal procedures of everyday life.

There are so many avenues of creativity. I am ready to join in that. There is a creativity waiting, there is an oversight waiting. This Congress is ready. I hope we go down in history as an oversight Congress. There are so many views, however, that I would not limit us to any one procedure.

DR. MILLER: There are surely many more opportunities to use market mechanisms in the regulatory process to reduce the cost of securing a given objective or of securing better objectives for a given cost. The chairman of the Council of Economic Advisers, Dr. Charles L. Schultze, has been an articulate spokesman for that point of view. Some of the volumes published by the American Enterprise Institute have also advocated this approach.

There are many opportunities for substantial advances. EPA's bubble concept is one important step, and I hope that regulatory agencies will adopt many more ideas of this kind.

SENATOR METZENBAUM: I would just say briefly that I could accept the concept of having an effluent charge or a pollution charge if the industry had no alternative but to pollute. Then perhaps, the industry would be charged enough to clean up the problem. I do not know whether it would work, but at least it is a novel enough idea to consider.

DR. MILLER: Dr. Robert Crandall, from the Brookings Institution, has responded to the criticism that effluent fees allow companies to "pollute for fee" by pointing out that the present system is "pollute for free." I think we can use market mechanisms and make substantial advances.

MR. DALY: This concludes another public policy forum presented by the American Enterprise Institute for Public Policy Research. On behalf of AEI, our hearty thanks to the distinguished and expert panelists, Mr. Mark J. Green, Senator Howard M. Metzenbaum, Senator Alan K. Simpson, and Dr. James C. Miller III. Our thanks also to our guests and experts in the audience for their participation.